A Dorling Kindersley Book

Text Terry Martin
Project Editor Mary Atkinson
US Editor Camela Decaire
Senior Art Editor Jane Horne
Deputy Managing Editor Mary Ling
Production Louise Barratt
Consultant Theresa Greenaway
Picture Researcher Lorna Ainger

Additional photography by Jane Burton,
Peter Chadwick, Gordon Clayton, Andy Crawford,
Philip Dowell, Andreas Einsiedel, Steve Gorton,
Frank Greenaway, Derek Hall, Colin Keates, Dave King,
Stephen Oliver, Tim Ridley, Karl Shone, Stephen Shott,
Kim Taylor, Matthew Ward, Jerry Young

Published in Canada in 1996
by Scholastic Canada Ltd.,
123 Newkirk Road,
Richmond Hill, Ontario L4C 3G5

First published in Great Britain in 1996
by Dorling Kindersley Limited,
9 Henrietta Street, London WC2E 8PS

Copyright © 1996 Dorling Kindersley Limited

Canadian Cataloguing in Publication Data

Martin, Terry, 1971–
Why are zebras black and white? : questions children ask about color

(Why books)
ISBN 0-590-24946-0

1. Color – Juvenile literature. I. Title. II. Series: Martin, Terry, 1971–   Why books.

QC495.5. M3 1996   j535.6   C96-931002-1

Color reproduction by Chromagraphics, Singapore. Printed and bound in Italy by L.E.G.O.
The publisher would like to thank the following for their kind permission to reproduce their
photographs: **Bruce Coleman Ltd.**: Hans Reinhard: (Why do bees . . . ?)c, (Why do flowers
have . . . ?)c; **The Image Bank**: Joe Van Os front cover c, (Why does the sky . . . ?)c, (Why do
zebras have . . . ?)c, Franklin Wagner Endpapers; **Natural History Photographic Agency**:
Haroldo Palo Jr. (Why are fruits always . . . ?)c; **Tony Stone Images**: Donovan Reese
(Why do leaves . . . ?)c, Stuart Westmorland back cover c, (Why is the sea blue, . . . ?)c

Questions

Why do things come in
lots of different colors?

Why does the sky turn
orange at sunset?

Why is the sea blue,
when water is clear?

Why do bees and hornets have
black and yellow stripes?

Why do zebras have
black and white stripes?

Why do leaves change
color in the fall?

Why do flowers have such
brightly colored petals?

Why are fruits always
such bright colors?

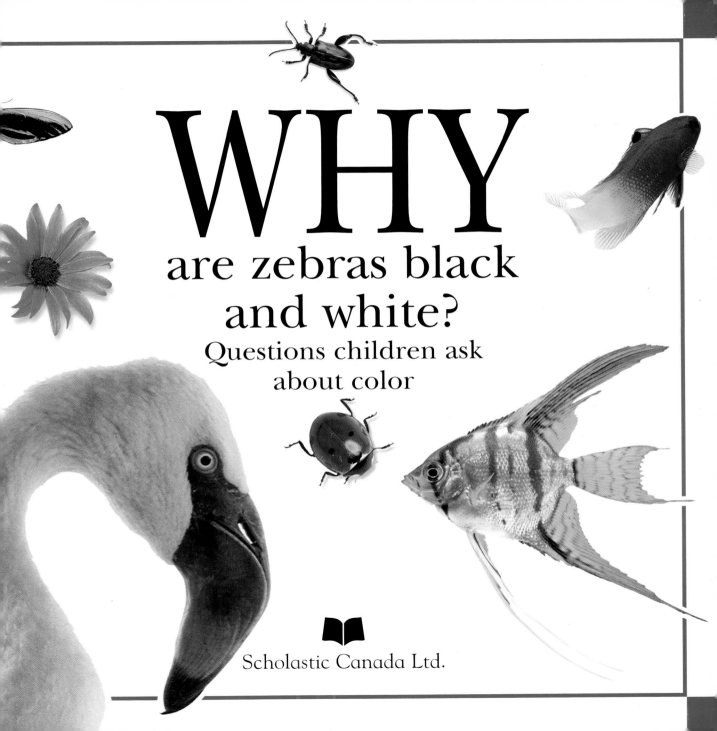

WHY

are zebras black and white?

Questions children ask about color

Scholastic Canada Ltd.

Why do things come

Most objects are colored by dyes or pigments. Dyes dissolve in water and color things like clothes, paper, even food. Pigments coat surfaces and are found in things like paint.

Why do I get orange when I mix red and yellow
All colors are mixtures of red, blue, and yellow. Try mixing red and blue paint. What color do you get?

n lots of different colors?

Why is my sweater red when sheep are white?
Sheep's wool is naturally most often white, but once it is shorn off, people can dye it any color they want – even pink with purple spots!

Why does the sky

As the sun sinks, its light travels through a long stretch of dusty air This air soaks up most of the light, leaving a fiery mix of red and orange

Why are pink flamingos pink?

Flamingos eat so many shrimps and other pink creatures that it's no wonder they're pink from beak to toe.

rn orange at sunset?

Why are butterflies such pretty colors?
One reason why butterflies have beautiful patterns on their wings is to help them recognize each other and so find a mate.

Why are parrots so brightly colored?
Parrots are some of nature's most startling creations. Their bold colors dazzle other parrots and warn enemies not to come too close.

Why is the sea blue,

Sunlight is a mix of colors, but when it hits the sea, all the colors except blue are absorbed by the water.

Why are tropical fish such beautiful colors?
Colorful patterns aren't just for show – they help these fish hide among their coral homes.

when water is clear?

Why are goldfish bright orange?
Goldfish used to be paler colors. But about 900 years ago, people started breeding the most colorful ones, creating brighter and brighter fish.

Why do lots of fish have silver scales?
Silver scales act like mirrors and reflect light, making fish hard to see from underneath.

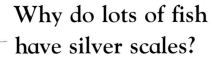

Why do bees and hornets

Once stung, twice shy! Yellow, black, and red are some of nature's warning colors. The stripes on bees and hornets warn birds of their painful stings.

Why do ladybugs have black spots?
Black spots on a red background warn all hungry creatures that these sweet-looking bugs release a nasty-smelling poison from their tiny knees.

have black and yellow stripes?

Why are some beetles shiny?
To us, many beetles look like sparkling jewels, but to their enemies, shiny colors sometimes say, "I'm poisonous."

Why do hoverflies look just like hornets?
This looks like a stinging hornet, but it's really a harmless hoverfly. Its black and yellow stripes trick hungry birds into thinking it can sting.

Why do zebras have black

The bold stripes on these zebras help the herd blend together, hiding them among the shadows at dusk. This confuses hungry lions searching for a meal.

Why are some cats striped?
Some cats have characteristics passed down from their wild ancestors, who often had stripes to help them hide while hunting.

nd white stripes?

Why do some insects look like leaves? In nature's game of hide and seek, birds search for tasty insects. They won't spot this cricket – its clever leaf disguise saves it from being a snack!

As a tree gets ready for winter, the green pigment in its leaves breaks up and useful chemicals pass back into the tree. Other pigments left behind include orange and red, which then color the leaves.

Why are leaves green?
Plants need the green pigment in their leaves to turn sunlight into life-giving energy.

change color in the fall?

Why are some trees always green?
Evergreen, or "forever green," trees have strong, thick leaves that can survive even cold, windy weather.

Why are lots of leaves shiny?
A waxy surface is like a leaf's coat, protecting it from wind, rain, and sun.

Why do flowers have suc

Flowers use color to attract birds, bees, and other creatures to taste their sweet nectar. The visitors leave behind pollen from other flowers – exactly what the plant needs to make its seeds.

Why are some flowers red?
To nectar-eating birds, a red flower is like a big, bright STOP sign. Birds see red clearly, so they won't miss these flowers.

brightly colored petals?

Why do some flowers have stripes?
Flower stripes are like landing lights on an airport runway. They guide bees to the nectar inside.

Why are some flowers yellow?
Bees get a buzz from yellow flowers. When they see yellow, they zoom down in search of nectar.

Why are fruits

Many plants grow colorful fruits to lure hungry creatures into eating them. The animals then spread the plants' seeds, found in the fruit, far and wide.

Why are peppers different colors?
Green peppers are unripe. When they ripen, they turn shades of yellow, orange, red, or other colors.

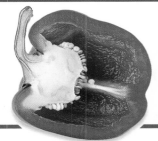

always such bright colors?

Why do I have to eat green vegetables?

"Eating green" isn't easy, but it's very important. Vegetables are full of the vitamins and minerals you need to grow tall and strong.

Why do apple cores turn brown?

Once you bite through the skin of an apple, reaches the soft flesh and turns it brown.

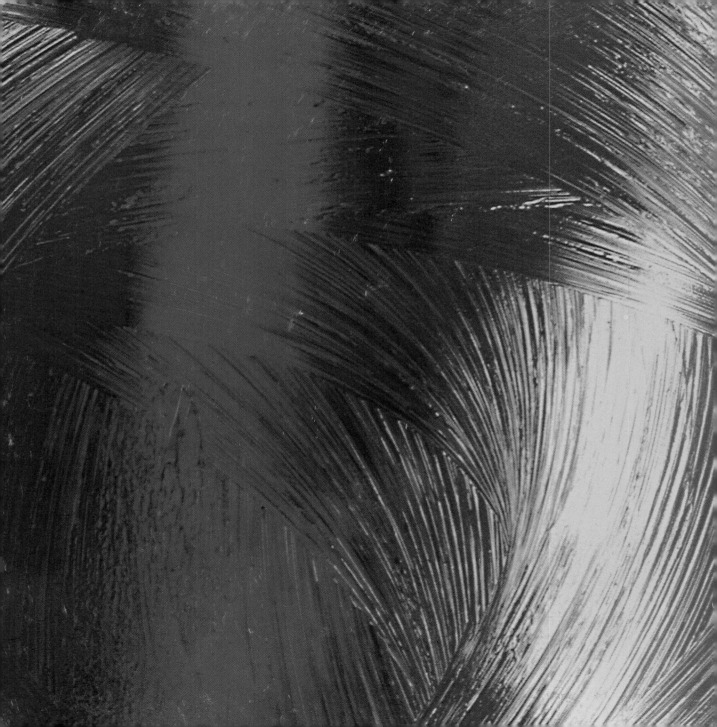